Unlimited Moments of Stillness

Glinda Foots; Linda Weathers

authorHOUSE®

AuthorHouse™
1663 Liberty Drive
Bloomington, IN 47403
www.authorhouse.com
Phone: 1 (800) 839-8640

Published by AuthorHouse 06/24/2016

ISBN: 978-1-5246-0726-5 (sc)
ISBN: 978-1-5246-0724-1 (hc)
ISBN: 978-1-5246-0725-8 (e)

Library of Congress Control Number: 2016907304

Print information available on the last page.

Any people depicted in stock imagery provided by Thinkstock are models, and such images are being used for illustrative purposes only. Certain stock imagery © Thinkstock.

This book is printed on acid-free paper.

Because of the dynamic nature of the Internet, any web addresses or links contained in this book may have changed since publication and may no longer be valid. The views expressed in this work are solely those of the author and do not necessarily reflect the views of the publisher, and the publisher hereby disclaims any responsibility for them.

Stillness

Stillness, you have given me a gift,
which continuously replenishes my wondering mind
with solutions for life's dilemmas.
In a world that is so bombarded
with elements of change,
coping and survivor necessities,
You calm my emotions.
My spirit is rejuvenated
each time I experience an intimate moment with you.
You connect me to who I am.
Through your unselfish, inseparable, passionate approach,
you bring depth to my understanding and solitude to my existence.
A vivid focus of the validity of my divine purpose in life unfolds.
Relaxation consumes my total self
with an outburst of renewed freeness, and
motivation to conquer life's challenges.
Stillness, you don't criticize me or point a finger.
The more I desire you, the more I linger.
This platinum relationship that we intimately share,
rekindles everything about me from the inside,
and makes way for an ultra-glow of warmth and happiness on my
surface.
Our relationship has made a great difference in the way I view life.
My thoughts are relentless. They travel at a high rate of speed.
I am consciously enlightened in my thinking,
and I'm grateful indeed.

I will baulk at even the thought of a negative force of interference,
and deter the company
of anyone who envies our relationship.
I will always utilize our togetherness
to rekindle my serenity.

I'm Lifted

My spirit was ignited with joy
By a small gesture of kindness—
rendered to me by an act of generosity.
Something small suddenly seemed large.
The ultimate unexpected gift
that I received lifted my spirit.
I experienced a feeling of ultimate joy!
I had to share my sense of overwhelming gratitude.
It enabled me to release the energy of excitement
That filled my heart.
I feel that the height of my spirit
Will enable me to endure some of the anxiety and pain
that have encased my heart.
I'm lifted.

Change of Heart

At first I was upset,
The big payback was set.
The way I was treated,
I felt hurt and defeated.
My mind was strong,
I planned strategies to do wrong.
It was time to get revenge you see,
For all the hurt and pain in me.
Then I remembered that I had a heart,
And how pure it was from the start.
So I snapped out of my depression,
Because I was headed toward regression.
Now I know for sure,
That my heart is pure.
I had a change of heart,
And decided to do my part.
I'll continue to do what I can,
And be an example for man.

Find Meaning in the Workplace

You can find meaning in the workplace
I'm talking to the whole human race
Take God with you from the start
And allow him to handle the major part
You may play a role too
Let it be what God allows you to do
Please don't take it upon yourself to do it all
Through this endeavor you will surely fall
It will cause you so much pain
Just allow God to guide you there is so much to gain
When there seems to be no hope
God will give you the skills to cope
When in your body the pain you feel
Your sickness he shall heal
When the earning potential diminishes
 Your finances he will replenish
When you fall out with your boss
And the working relationship is at a loss
God will step right in and mend your heart
And never again will disagreements start
Don't question the foundation of your belief
It's through faith that you get relief
So ask God to stick around on your job everyday
It's through his guidance you will get full pay

My Journey

Waiting patiently—
Enthralled and undaunted,
Yet totally secure in my focus.
Will I prevail in harmony with my journey's direction?
Divinely so.

Run Away Child

Run away child
If you must
But run away in a direction
That you totally trust
Run away to peace
Run away to people
Who have your best interest at heart
Run away to success
Run away—to a better you
And if by chance you get lost along the way—
Search inside yourself and start over again
Run away child—
To a better you
Run away to you
Who understand defeat
Just to start over again—
And endure to the end
Run away from hurt and pain—
By realizing that joy is yours to gain
Run away from bad company—
That means you no good
And hope that one day—
Your actions will be understood
As you are running away—
Don't look back
Far beyond the sunset
Lies your true dream

REACH

Do not allow deterrents to
deprive you of the key to
success that is residually yours
Reach higher than your height
Travel farther than the distance
 Focus in light instead of darkness
Enter into your open door

Loving Life

I'm loving life because I changed my ways,
I do things differently these days.
Problems yeah I've had enough,
I can't be bothered with negative stuff.
People are depressed for no reason,
My life is headed to a new season.
The best attire I will wear in style,
I will travel and relax for a while.
A breath of fresh air is headed my way,
I'll chill with happiness each day.

Losing a Loved One

When you lose a loved one
You gain ownership of the key
To their everlasting spirit
Through memories
The loving moments you shared
Were molded into a masterpiece
Of eternal love
The sacred memories will bring you
Continuous joy and solace.
You are an intimate part of
A Great Unity

Rock Bottom

I've hit rock bottom before
And thought I couldn't go on anymore
But a voice whispered inside
And suggested that I swallow my pride
For it was I who had to decide
What it took for me to survive
To pay the bills and to make ends meet
I had to press forward and conquer defeat
Many tears I shed during this ordeal
But I kept striving and didn't miss a meal
I borrowed money from here and there
And got food from almost anywhere
There was a drive inside of me
That kept pushing and wouldn't let me be
Will power came from somewhere
It was God I know he was there
Keep your focus the voice said
As it rang inside my head
So I made up my mind to do just that
There has been so much progress I've made a comeback
Now I'm clutching along still
Climbing that rugged hill
Green grass is peaking down at me
And I'm determined to be all I can be
So many opportunities have come my way
Bright ideas keep coming everyday
The lesson I learned a few years ago
Is valuable to me and I know

That no matter how long it takes
Regardless to my misfortunes and mistakes
I will succeed in my endeavor
And I promise to give up never

Job Change

When you change directions
From one job to the next
You will be transferred
To the highway of success
The traffic will not stop your progress
For you will speed to the position
That's in the right lane for you

A Kind Gesture

Take the time to plant a seed.
A kind gesture is all you need.
Allow your actions to cultivate.
Uplift a spirit-increase someone's faith.
Your inner peace will be a bond of hope.
Create a legacy-A vision in scope.

Shackled Emotions

You are shackled by your emotions.
You are out of control, and seem unable to let go.
Your stress level has risen—you are not free anymore.
Situations, which you cannot control,
Consume your peaceful, serene spirit,
Your happiness is smothered.
Release the shackles—
Free your spirit from distress,
Disconsolation, and deeply rooted Emotional Pain!

Dancing Happiness

I saw happiness dance today
I was in awe and couldn't find the words to say
You can't imagine how I felt inside
These were true feelings I could not hide
How grateful I felt for my accomplishments in life
Although I toiled through misery and strife
Sometimes working menial jobs for pay
I kept working anyway
Knowing that I had to cope
I still had great hope
With biases and unfairness too
I kept pressing on because I had a job to do
Now my job is my true passion
And I perform it in high fashion
My advice to you still remains
No matter what the suffering or pain
Strive to be the best you can be
It can be done look at me

Calmness

A sea of beauty is before me.
The waves of bravery are within me.
My strokes of strength surround me.
My anchor of desire penetrates the depth of my soul.
My inner soul is filled with calmness.

So Much to Deal With

There is so much to deal with in a day
We must strive to cope anyway
When things get out of hand
There will be so much in demand
Just push forward and see the light
Everything will be alright
People have a special touch
We are programmed to do so much
When you are determined to do your best
Keep striving—just stop to rest to
Find peace in what you do
That is the thing that will see you through
Treat everybody the way you should
Give a smile if you would
Sometimes life is a pain
When it's difficult there is rain
Try to hang tough
Although you've had enough
Don't give up—just stick to life's test
Give each day your best
Be an example for people you meet
Make your personality hard to beat
A role model is one that you adore
Make yourself visible and seek no more
So deal with obstacles that hit you in the face
You are not alone while you run this race
Be of good cheer and don't sweat life's blows
They will be over as progress flows

Free Your Mind

A free mind
Is like a sweet breeze of
crystallized air.
Its focused path
will guide you through
your obstacles of distress.
Free your mind
and experience the
FREEDOM.

Dare To Heal

Life is filled with disappointments
that will lure your happiness away.
But through His goodness and grace,
He'll give you joy each day.
Although you've gone through trying times,
And devastation too—
Dare to heal, no matter what your situation—
He's always there for you.
You possess an inner strength—
God gave it to us all.
That strength will lift you up—
Even if you stumble, you won't fall.
You will encounter many problems—
Heartaches and pain too.
But God will help you with life's challenges—
He's able to pull you through.
Releasing the pain and sorrow
May seem to be a chore.
But just Dare to heal
And vow to hurt no more.
Remain optimistic—
Look on the bright side.
Release the pain that is within your heart—
And allow peace to abide.

Direction of the Mind

It is not so much the direction of the wind
that directs one's sail,
but the direction in which the mind embarks upon
as an impacting result.

Today

I wonder not about tomorrow
But of my destiny for today
Which way will I wander
Which way will I sway
What message from within
Will my heart convey
There is certainty in my fate
For which I surely believe
Whatever my journey for today
Will transpire indeed

New Year's Resolution

My New Year's Resolution will be different this year,
I am going to face life without fear.
I used to make a resolution just to go through the motion,
But the one I make this year will be given my full devotion.
Those petty things that I hold in my heart,
I am going to clear them out to get a fresh start.
I have goals to complete,
I will complete them without defeat.
I will pray for my enemies and my friends,
A wound heals and a heart mends.
I will mind my own business and do as I please,
I will live life to the fullest and I'll do it with ease.
My resolution will not be placed on a shelf,
I will fulfill my promise to myself.
Life is a challenge and I'll pass the test,
When this year is over, I will have done my best.

Fly

Soar
Into the next phase of your life
With a purpose
Each opportunity
With the possibility of success
Is waiting for you
To take wings and
Fly

Something Is Brewing

Something is brewing for you
Take your life
To the next level
Don't stop
You've got to reach the top
And if you get tired on the way
Rest don't quit
Success is brewing for you

It's not over yet
You have a chance
To do more in your life
Start now
And when things go wrong
Please be strong
Something is brewing for you
Success is brewing for you

Am I Good Enough

Am I good enough to rise above poverty?
Am I good enough to deserve greatness?
Am I good enough to become successful?
Am I good enough to be considered good enough?
I am.
I am good enough to be a vessel for success.
Just like those who have preceded me—
Like those deserving who will follow in my footsteps.
I am good enough to achieve greatness.
I am good enough to succeed!
I am good enough to be considered good enough!
I Am Good Enough!

You

You are the proud owner
of the key to happiness.
You are the deserving recipient of the key
to another great opportunity.
You are the owner of the key
to a new beginning in
Leadership
Education
Friendship
Love.

Weary Eyes

Through my weary eyes
I saw no bright tomorrow
I pondered in my quest for direction
Then,
through my weary eyes
The sun peered

Establish Your Life

Establish your life and take action,
Explore all avenues to suit your satisfaction.
From being responsible to owning a car,
You are not a failure by far.
Elevate your mind to a higher plain,
Leave no room for doubt to remain.
Circumstances will be better than before,
Don't allow stress to get you down anymore.
Life is a puzzle and each piece must fit,
Assemble success and enjoy every bit.

Positive Attitude

My Positive attitude is
The driving force
Toward my success.
It keeps me from
Thinking, saying, or doing
Things
That may impede
Progress in my endeavors.

Discovered Treasure

As I walked along the seashore
I discovered a treasure that
I had never seen before—Joy
For it was buried deeply into
My sand of emotions

Country Road

I traveled a country road today.
En route to my destination,
I saw creations that I've never seen before.
Each had a distinct uniqueness,
which made the distinguished difference
in their contribution toward
earthly beauty.

Encouraged

Each day I'm encouraged to
Consult With God,
See the good in myself and others,
Put on my brightest smile,
Tackle my fears,
Overcome my obstacles,
Put forth my best effort,
Take my biggest step,
Then call it a day.

Rise to the Occasion

When defeat is only a mental deterrent
And your will power is almost gone
Dig deeper into your soul
Rise to the occasion and hold on
Grab your desire and don't let go
For endless opportunities are somewhere waiting
For you to let victory show

Inflamed Love

My heart beats faster
when inflamed
with the flamboyant fire
from our unspoken desires.
Receiving the spark
from your diamond of love
creates in me
 a river of flooding,
uncontrollable passion
that is molded into a rock
of everlasting togetherness.

I Rescued A Dove

I rescued a dove.
It was entangled in a bout with fate,
which caused trouble and distress.
It was wounded in spirit,
and cried out through silent pain.
As I encountered the dove,
I noticed the depth of its pain,
and the appearance of its wounded body.
I anchored myself by its side—
Nourishing the wounds—
Both, its spirit and flesh.
I felt a part of the pain engulf my spirit.
I attended to the dove
with kind words and motivation
toward a better tomorrow.
The dove flapped its wings and
responded to me with a
desire for a new found hope for recovery.
Its wounds could have been prevented
with just a simple act of concern and love.
The dove's heart was in agony and pain
until harsh reality gave it
a pain pill of optimism.

The Power of Prayer

I believe in the power of prayer
People need it everywhere
Sunday I prayed in church
My request to God was needed so much
For it was Him I tried to reach
Before I heard the minister preach
I focused on my request at hand
I knew God would understand
So I bowed my head and pleaded my case
I whispered the words at my own pace
Afterward I held my head up high
I looked toward heaven and gave a sigh
I had faith bigger than a mustard seed
I knew God would answer my prayer indeed

The Sun

The sun is shining brighter
Than I have ever seen
It's as if the sky gave way
Just to rejoice
Now I know exactly
What it means
To have light after darkness

Who am I

I matter in society.
I am important.
I am a work of art.
I am designed for greatness.
I am engraved in the universe.
I matter because of my intellect.
I am confident and I will succeed.
I am dedicated to mankind.
I am a force to be reckoned with.
I am…and I will forever be…

God Made a Difference

When God made me
He made a difference
In the way I am
The way I walk
The way I talk
The way I think
What I'm really trying to say is
God
Made
Me Different

My Long Lost Love

I allowed myself to depreciate
Lowered my glamorous standards and ate
Consumed more calories than I needed
To my sweet tooth—I gladly heeded
I lost track of the count
Continued to eat in large amounts
Had no shame in what I did
I gained some inches around the mid
Couldn't feel the pain nor see the gain
I heeded to food in the fast lane
Exercise I valued less
My will power was put to rest
Was I able to endure
My love for eating made sure
Soon came the time
For me to relax and unwind
I tried on my clothes—I wanted to go out
But they were too small—couldn't go that route
My weight had gotten out of control
I thought I could handle it—I was bold
But my self-esteem started to fade
And so did my pride—it even swayed
Started to isolate myself
Felt that I had nothing left
I had to buy my clothes bigger
Had lost my shape and my figure
Discovered my weight had gone wild
It cramped my pride and my style
This couldn't be true I sighed

I weighed on a scale that really lied
Started to eat less
I was fed up with this mess
What are my chances of getting skinny
My chances are as good as any
I'm tired of looking blimpie
Feeling depressed and oh so wimpy
Who would want to look like this
Glamorous outings I didn't want to miss
I encountered friends who were still looking good
With a few months of dieting—I knew I could
I started to work out—couldn't wait to run
Got tired very easily—it was no fun
Temptation nipped at my desire
I stayed strong and declared it a liar
As I controlled my caloric intake
I stayed in the mirror and watched my weight
Finally I was becoming a little slimmer
My lost hope for beauty was dimmer
Tried on some clothes that finally fit
I started to scream—this is it
No longer will I be the laughing stock
For I own the key and control the lock
Of how I exercise and eat
My love for food I will defeat
Now—I'm looking good and feeling great
No longer will I wag unnecessary weight
For this love was lost and I finally see
I had it all the time inside of me

Don't Stress About It

You'll always have problems in your life
Constantly knocking at your door
It's amazing how they seem to find you
No matter where you go
You'll find yourself
Sitting around with your head hanging down
Trying to find an answer to your problem
Don't stress about it
There is a solution to your problem
Try your best to solve it
Then—release it and let it go

Search for Fulfillment

My search for fulfillment
Has gone wild!
I am on a mission
To identify my true passion.
It is through the jungle of meditation
That I will discover it
And explore my options for Happiness.

The Towering Mind

A mind geared
Toward the stars
Filled with inspiration
Grasping for those things
Dreamed about long ago
Those things that are the focal point
To success
Seeking for productive thoughts
Those thoughts that will construct
Other minds toward higher magnitude
Those thoughts that are Immovable

America (written on September 11, 2001)

America is strong
We must hold on
To the beliefs and treasures
Our forefathers have given us
We will try with all we have
To uphold the American Dream
And let our flag reflect
What our nation believes

When Opposition comes our way
We will grow stronger day by day
And when we need a helping hand
We will call on God
He understands
America we love you
We'll always be faithful to you
America we love you
We'll always be loyal to you

America has changed
We must remain
True and loyal to America
She needs us
In spite of all that we've been through
We will try our hardest to do
Whatever it takes to heal
The wounded in spirit

Statue of Nature

There on a mountain
Rigid with layers of bark
Stood a statue of nature
Well formed with natural
Earthly accessories
Its prized possessions
Are restored yearly
The inward beauty
Remains in state
Until springtime
Its sole purpose is for
Nature's sake

Day Dream

Dream while it is day
Allow your actions to
Take you
To that place you have
Never gone before
To do those things you
Have hoped for
Dream of reality
Know that your aspirations
Will be fulfilled

Now I know

Now I know why I experience bitterness and sweetness
This combination of life's situations
Will blend together
To make sense of what life should taste like

The Idle Homestead

Along the lonely road
Sat a deserted dwelling
Hidden with
Grass-grown scenery
Useless-
Yet so valuable
With stored memories
Of yesteryears-

Stillness

Stillness
I'll never let you go
Stillness
You take my breath away
You calm my emotions
You connect me to who I am
When I'm in your presence
All I think of is peace
While engulfed in silence
I listen to my spirit
I find comfort from within
To sustain me day by day
There is no greater feeling
Than when I allow you
To take total control
You caress my spirit with desire
And the unspeakable unfolds

Build Your Dream

Build your dream
Build it to last
Make haste
Time travels fast

Choose a dream
One which is in demand
Select it from your heart
Your bright future is at hand

Focus on your desire
Lay a foundation for happiness
Frame your dream
And then construct success

Build your dream
Reach for the sky
In order to choose your unique star
You must soar high

When you choose
 Your unique star
Let it shine brightly
Both near and far

Mold and shape your future
From the depth of your soul
Even when you encounter problems
And when dilemmas unfold

Opportunities are like open doors
Enter with a determined mind
Carve greatness and endurance
Lost chances are hard to find

Challenge your mind
To build a dream that will make you proud
Believe deeply in your ability
Failure should not be allowed

Distress or interference
May knock at your door
Don't welcome distractors
But seek success even more

Follow your blueprint
Use your solid foundation as you need
Empower others when you build your dream
And enjoy a fulfilled life indeed

Unlimited Moments of Stillness Photo Gallery

.

Printed in the United States
By Bookmasters